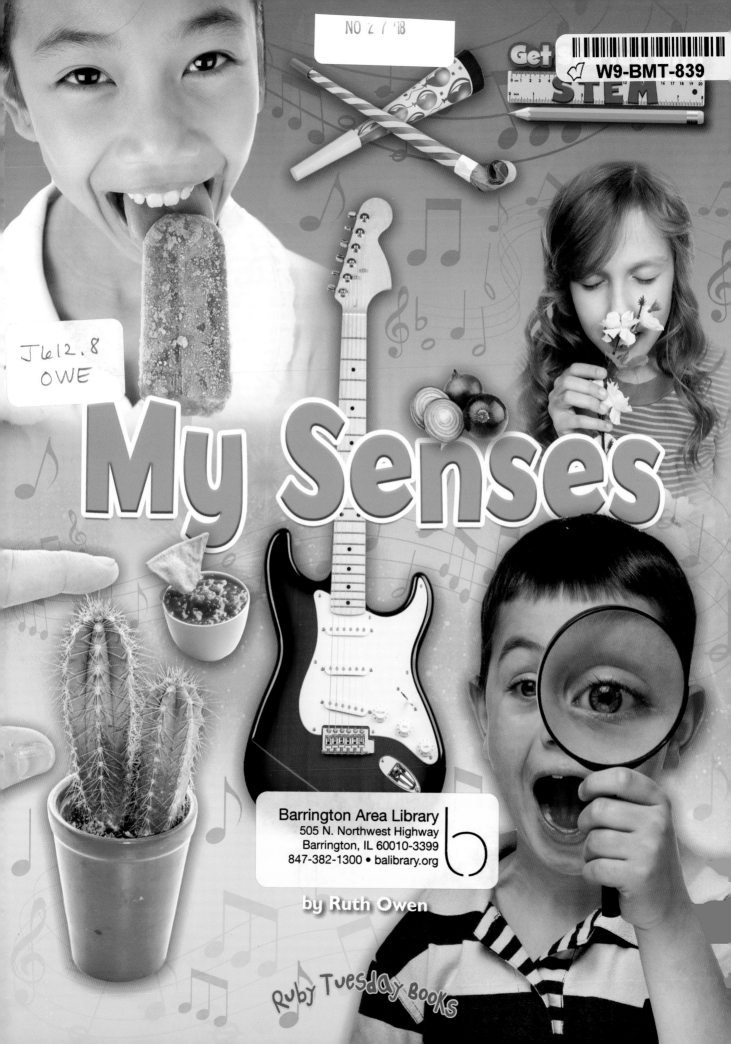

My Senses

Get STEM

by Ruth Owen

Ruby Tuesday Books

Published in 2017 by Ruby Tuesday Books Ltd.

Editor: Mark J. Sachner
Designer: Emma Randall
Consultant: Judy Wearing, PhD, BEd
Production: John Lingham

Photo credits:
Alamy: 8 (bottom), 12, 16, 21 (top); Science Photo Library: 11; Shutterstock: Cover, 1, 2–3, 4–5, 6–7, 8 (top), 9, 10, 13, 14–15, 17, 18–19, 20, 21 (bottom), 22–23, 24–25, 26–27, 28–29, 30–31.

Library of Congress Control Number: 2016918445

ISBN 978-1-911341-39-0

Printed and published in the United States of America

For further information including rights and permissions requests, please contact our Customer Service Department at 877-337-8577.

Contents

Words shown in **bold** in the text are explained in the glossary.

The download button shows there are free worksheets or other resources available. Go to:

www.rubytuesdaybooks.com/getstarted

Enjoying Your World

When you visit a park on a summer day, you feel warm sun on your skin.

You might see brightly colored flowers and hear...

...bees buzzing.

You might smell newly mowed grass and enjoy the taste of a delicious sandwich.

All this is possible because of your senses.

Let's Talk

Your five senses are seeing, hearing, smelling, tasting, and touching. Which body parts do you use for each of your senses?

How We See

We use our eyes to see the world around us. In order to see, we need light.

Light from the Sun

Light travels into your eyes, where special **cells** send messages to your brain.

Your brain turns the messages into images that you see.

Light from flashlights and lamps

Your Eye Up Close

Each of your eyeballs is about the size of a ping-pong ball.

Eyelid

Pupil

Iris

Sclera

Every time you blink, your eyelids clean your eyes and moisten them so they don't get dry.

The pupil is a small round opening. Light enters your eye through the pupil.

The iris can be brown, blue, or green.

The sclera is the white part of your eye.

Some people have trouble seeing clearly. Usually they can improve their sight by wearing glasses or **contact lenses**.

Millions of Colors

Your eyes can see movement, shapes, and about 10 million different colors!

Inside your eyes are tiny cells called rods and cones.

In each eye you have about 7 million cone cells that help you to see colors. You also have about 120 million rod cells that help you to see in dim light.

Let's Explore

A color can be bright or pale. It can also come in many different shades.

Choose one of the colors below.

Red   Blue   Green

Yellow   Pink   Orange

How many objects can you find in your home or classroom in different shades of that color?

Can you invent a new color?

Gather your equipment:
- A notebook and pen
- Liquid paints
- A small plate
- An eyedropper
- Teaspoons

1. Start by thinking about colors.

What colors do you like best? Will your new color be bright or pale?

Other people might want to use your new color. So record every step in your notebook to make a color recipe.

2. Begin by putting a teaspoon of paint on the plate.

3. Next, add a second color with a clean teaspoon or the eyedropper. Keep adding and mixing until your color is just right.

What will you call the new color?

4. Now follow your recipe and make the color again.

Does it look the same? If not, what did you do differently?

Super Sight

Our eyes are usually able to see very tiny things, such as ants or grains of sand.

Magnifying glass

We can also use a **microscope** or a magnifying glass to help us see tiny objects.

Let's Investigate!

Try looking at these different objects through a magnifying glass.

- Your fingertip
  Can you see the lines that make up your fingerprint?

- Coins
  What does the picture on a coin show?

- Sand
  Are all the sand grains the same color?

- A flower
  What parts can you see? Is there a pattern in the flower's center?

Sand

Flower center

These pictures show some everyday objects seen through a microscope.
Can you guess what they are?

You might find ▶ **A**
this on your
clothes or shoes.

You will find this in
the bathroom.
▼

B

People put this on
their food. ▶ **C**

(The answers are at the bottom of the page.)

Answers: A is a hook and loop fastener, such as Velcro. **B** is toilet paper. **C** is salt and pepper.

11

Sounds All Around

We hear sounds with our ears.
But what exactly are sounds?

When you strum the strings of a ukulele, it makes them **vibrate**, or move back and forth.

Sound waves

The movement creates vibrations, called sound waves, that travel through the air.

If you slam a door or bang a drum, this creates vibrations of air, or sound waves, too. All sounds are invisible vibrations of air.

The part of your ear that sticks out is called the auricle.

It collects sound waves from the air.

Auricle

Let's Talk

How does sound make life more fun? How is it helpful in your life?

Inside Your Ears

Once sound waves are inside your ear, they vibrate your eardrum.

Your eardrum passes on the vibrations to three tiny bones.

Eardrum

Tiny bones

Cochlea

Sound waves

The bones pass the vibrations to a part of your ear called the cochlea.

Finally, the cochlea sends messages to your brain and you hear a sound.

This picture shows the size of the three tiny bones in your ear compared to a pencil tip. They are the smallest bones in your body.

Incus

Stapes

Malleus

Let's Design It!

Can you design a musical instrument that makes sounds?

1. Begin by thinking about your design.

How will you play the instrument to make it vibrate? For example, will you strum it, bang it, or shake it?

What materials could you use?

Draw a picture of your instrument design in a notebook.

2. Gather your materials and make your design.

How would you describe the sound it makes?

What can you do to make the sound louder or quieter?

Can you make the sound higher or deeper?

What will you call your new instrument?

Helpful Hearing

Your sense of hearing helps keep you safe.

Your ears can hear cars and other traffic.

They can also hear a fire alarm or someone shouting a warning.

Hearing aid

Some people have **hearing loss**. They might wear a **hearing aid** to improve their hearing.

There are sounds all around us, but we don't always notice them.

Let's investigate what sounds we hear outdoors by drawing a sound map.

1. Take a notebook and pencils outside to a yard, garden, park, or your school playground. Draw yourself in the center of the map.

2. Listen for the sounds around you. Draw an arrow to where each sound comes from and draw what you hear.

Your Nose

What do freshly baked cookies, flowers, and old shoes have in common? They all have smells.

Nostrils

As you breathe in air through your nostrils, these smells enter your nose.

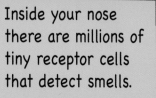

Inside your nose there are millions of tiny receptor cells that detect smells.

Once your nose detects a smell, it sends a message to your brain.

In less than a second, your brain figures out what the smell is.

Yuck! Stinky shoes.

Let's Talk

How does your sense of smell help keep you safe?

Let's Investigate!

Use your sense of smell to make a garden scent pot.

Gather your equipment:
- A small plastic pot with a lid
- A spoon
- Water

1. Explore a garden and its scents, or smells, such as flowers, leaves, herbs, bark, or soil.

2. Collect samples of leaves, flowers, or other materials in your pot. Add water to the pot.

3. Mix or crush the materials to help bring out their scents.

How would you describe the smell in your pot?

4. Put the lid on your pot and leave it overnight.

Does it smell different the next day? In what way?

BE CAREFUL!
Ask permission before collecting flowers or leaves. Wash your hands with warm water and soap after touching materials in a garden or yard.

Keeping You Safe

Your sense of smell helps to keep you safe.

If your nose breathes in smoke, your brain recognizes the smell.

It tells you something is burning, and this can sometimes mean danger.

When milk has gone bad, your sense of smell stops you from drinking it and possibly getting ill.

Scientists think your nose can detect about one trillion different smells.

Let's Explore!

How many different smells can you recognize?

Take a notebook and pen and go on a smell safari along your street, around your home or yard, or in your school playground or a park.

As you walk, make a note of the things you smell.

How many smells did your nose detect?

Which was the worst smell?

Which was the nicest smell?

Get Tasting!

When it's time to eat or drink, your senses go into action.

Before you even take a bite, your eyes see the food and your nose smells it.

This makes your mouth start producing a slimy liquid called **saliva**, or spit.

Once you take a bite, your teeth and tongue work together to mix the food with saliva.

As your tongue helps mash up the food, it detects the food's flavors.

Your mouth produces up to 2 quarts (2 liters) of saliva every day. If your tongue is dry, it cannot taste very well. So saliva keeps your tongue wet.

Tastes and Taste Buds

Your tongue is covered with microscopic bumps, called papillae. Some of the papillae contain taste buds.

There are about 10,000 taste buds on your tongue.

This close-up picture of a tongue was taken by a powerful microscope.

The taste buds are on here.

Papillae

Taste buds detect flavors in your food. The information gathered by your taste buds is sent to your brain.

Your brain receives
the messages, and
in an instant you
taste the flavor.

Let's Explore

Savory

Mushrooms

Fish
sticks

Cheese

Sour

Sour cream

Grapes

Lemons

Bitter

Dark chocolate

Coffee

Red cabbage

All the foods we eat can be sorted into
five different types of flavors: sour,
sweet, bitter, salty, and savory.

What are your favorite foods?

**Which of the taste groups do your
favorite foods belong to?**

Sweet

Ice cream

Milk
chocolate

Honey

Salty

Bacon

Chips

POP
CORN

Popcorn

25

Taste Teamwork

Your nose is on your taste team, too. Before you even put your food into your mouth, your nose can smell it.

Once you are chewing, more smells travel from your mouth up into your nose.

If something tastes bad, your sense of taste warns you that the food or drink might harm you.

Then your nose sends all this information to your brain.

Together, your nose, taste buds, and brain give you your sense of taste.

Be a Scientist!

How does food taste if you can't smell it? Let's investigate!

Gather your equipment:
- Some samples of food (see below)
- A scarf or blindfold
- An adult helper
- A glass of water

1. Ask your adult helper to secretly prepare eight small samples of foods that you like.

2. Put on the blindfold, or keep your eyes tightly closed so you can't see the samples.

3. Hold your nose tight so you can't smell, and ask your helper to give you a food sample to taste.

What does the food taste like? Can you guess what it is?

4. Taste all the other samples and try to guess what they are. You might want to take a mouthful of water between each one.

How many samples did you guess correctly?

What do your results tell you about taste and your sense of smell?

Sometimes you can't taste your food when you have a cold. Why do you think this is?

(The answer is at the bottom of the page.)

Answer: When you have a cold, your taste buds keep working, but your blocked nose can't smell your food.

27

Your Sense of Touch

Every day, your sense of touch allows you to feel things with your skin.

Beneath the outer layer of your skin are millions of cells called touch receptors.

Prickly

Hot

Cold

When you touch an object with your fingers, the touch receptors in your skin detect how it feels.

They send messages to your brain, and you instantly feel the object's temperature and **texture**.

Squishy

Rough

Woolly

Let's Test It!

How good is your sense of touch?

Find a jigsaw with four to eight pieces.

Close your eyes and try to do the jigsaw just by feeling the shapes of the pieces.

Hot, Cold, and Ouch!

If you touch something hot or sharp, your sense of touch helps protect you. How?

The touch receptor cells in your skin send a message to your brain that your hand is in danger.

In an instant, you feel pain, so you stop touching and stay safe!

Your hands are very sensitive because the skin has more touch receptor cells than other parts of your body.

Your mouth and tongue also have touch receptors that help you feel heat and cold.

They warn you if your food is too hot and will burn your mouth.

Let's Explore

Get creative with your sense of touch and make a textures board.

Gather your equipment:
- A big square of thick cardboard
- A black marker pen and ruler
- Strong glue
- Nine materials with different textures

1. Divide the cardboard into nine sections, using the ruler and marker pen.

2. Glue a different material to each section. Be creative!

3. Test your friends' sense of touch by asking them to close their eyes and touch the board.

How many of the different materials can your friends identify by using their sense of touch?

Glossary

cells (SELZ)
Very tiny parts of a living thing. Your bones, skin, hair, and every part of you are made of cells.

contact lenses
(KON-takt LEN-ziz)
Small see-through discs that some people wear on their eyes to help improve their sight.

hearing aid (HEER-ing AYD)
A small piece of equipment that is worn on the outside of the ear and helps make sounds louder.

hearing loss (HEER-ing LAWSS)
Being unable to hear some sounds or all sounds. Some people are born with hearing loss. Some people lose their hearing because of an injury or illness.

microscope (MYE-kruh-skope)
A piece of equipment used for seeing things that are too small to see with your eyes alone.

saliva (suh-LYE-vuh)
A clear liquid in the mouth that helps us chew, taste, and swallow.

texture (TEKS-chur)
How the surface of something feels, for example, smooth or rough.

vibrate (VYE-brate)
To make shaking movements back and forth or from side to side.

Index